Archie loves Betty and Veronica MAD LIBS®

written by Paul Kupperberg
concept created by Roger Price & Leonard Stern

PSS!
PRICE STERN SLOAN
An Imprint of Penguin Group (USA) LLC

PRICE STERN SLOAN
Published by the Penguin Group
Penguin Group (USA) LLC, 375 Hudson Street, New York, New York 10014, USA

USA | Canada | UK | Ireland | Australia | New Zealand | India | South Africa | China

penguin.com
A Penguin Random House Company

Published by Price Stern Sloan, a division of Penguin Young Readers Group,
345 Hudson Street, New York, New York 10014.
Printed in the USA.

ISBN 978-0-8431-8114-2

1 3 5 7 9 10 8 6 4 2

MAD LIBS
INSTRUCTIONS

MAD LIBS® is a game for people who don't like games! It can be played by one, two, three, four, or forty.

● RIDICULOUSLY SIMPLE DIRECTIONS

In this tablet you will find stories containing blank spaces where words are left out. One player, the READER, selects one of these stories. The READER does not tell anyone what the story is about. Instead, he/she asks the other players, the WRITERS, to give him/her words. These words are used to fill in the blank spaces in the story.

● TO PLAY

The READER asks each WRITER in turn to call out a word—an adjective or a noun or whatever the space calls for—and uses them to fill in the blank spaces in the story. The result is a MAD LIBS® game.

When the READER then reads the completed MAD LIBS® game to the other players, they will discover that they have written a story that is fantastic, screamingly funny, shocking, silly, crazy, or just plain dumb—depending upon which words each WRITER called out.

● EXAMPLE (*Before* and *After*)

"_____!" he said _____
         EXCLAMATION   ADVERB

as he jumped into his convertible _____ and
                                      NOUN

drove off with his _____ wife.
                     ADJECTIVE

"_____*Ouch*_____!" he said _____*stupidly*_____
         EXCLAMATION   ADVERB

as he jumped into his convertible _____*cat*_____ and
                                  NOUN

drove off with his _____*brave*_____ wife.
                   ADJECTIVE

MAD☺LIBS®
QUICK REVIEW

In case you have forgotten what adjectives, adverbs, nouns, and verbs are, here is a quick review:

An ADJECTIVE describes something or somebody. *Lumpy, soft, ugly, messy,* and *short* are adjectives.

An ADVERB tells how something is done. It modifies a verb and usually ends in "ly." *Modestly, stupidly, greedily,* and *carefully* are adverbs.

A NOUN is the name of a person, place, or thing. *Sidewalk, umbrella, bridle, bathtub,* and *nose* are nouns.

A VERB is an action word. *Run, pitch, jump,* and *swim* are verbs. Put the verbs in past tense if the directions say PAST TENSE. *Ran, pitched, jumped,* and *swam* are verbs in the past tense.

When we ask for A PLACE, we mean any sort of place: a country or city (*Spain, Cleveland*) or a room (*bathroom, kitchen*).

An EXCLAMATION or SILLY WORD is any sort of funny sound, gasp, grunt, or outcry, like *Wow!, Ouch!, Whomp!, Ick!,* and *Gadzooks!*

When we ask for specific words, like a NUMBER, a COLOR, an ANIMAL, or a PART OF THE BODY, we mean a word that is one of those things, like *seven, blue, horse,* or *head.*

When we ask for a PLURAL, it means more than one. For example, *cat* pluralized is *cats.*

MAD LIBS® is fun to play with friends, but you can also play it by yourself! To begin with, DO NOT look at the story on the page below. Fill in the blanks on this page with the words called for. Then, using the words you have selected, fill in the blank spaces in the story.

Now you've created your own hilarious MAD LIBS® game!

EENIE-MEENIE-MINIE-GO!

VERB (PAST TENSE) _____

TYPE OF FOOD _____

ADJECTIVE _____

VERB _____

ADVERB _____

VEHICLE _____

VERB _____

PLURAL NOUN _____

NOUN _____

VERB ENDING IN "ING" _____

NOUN _____

ADJECTIVE _____

ADJECTIVE _____

VERB _____

MAD☺LIBS®
EENIE-MEENIE-MINIE-GO!

Moose _____ into Pop's Chocklit Shoppe, where
      VERB (PAST TENSE)

Jughead and Reggie were sharing a plate of _____ at the
                  TYPE OF FOOD

counter. "You guys hear the _____ gossip about Archie?"
                  ADJECTIVE

Moose asked. "Yeah, he said he's in big trouble and has to _____
                         VERB

town . . . _____!" Jughead answered. "Did he crash his
      ADVERB

_____ this morning and is afraid his dad's gonna
VEHICLE

_____ him?" Reggie wondered. "I heard he ran over Mr.
VERB

Lodge's prize _____ with a lawn mower!" Moose said. Just
      PLURAL NOUN

then, they looked out the _____ and saw Archie
                  NOUN

_____ by with a packed _____ in his hands.
VERB ENDING IN "ING"   NOUN

"Trying to run from your dad and Mr. Lodge, pal?" Jughead asked. "It's

more _____ than that," Archie moaned. "Tomorrow is
    ADJECTIVE

Valentine's Day and since I can't choose between taking out Betty or

Veronica, I figured the _____ thing to do is _____
           ADJECTIVE   VERB

somewhere safe until it's over!"

From ARCHIE® LOVES BETTY AND VERONICA® MAD LIBS® • TM and © 2014 Archie Comic Publications, Inc.
Published by Price Stern Sloan, an imprint of Penguin Group (USA) LLC, 345 Hudson Street, New York, NY 10014.

MAD LIBS® is fun to play with friends, but you can also play it by yourself! To begin with, DO NOT look at the story on the page below. Fill in the blanks on this page with the words called for. Then, using the words you have selected, fill in the blank spaces in the story.

Now you've created your own hilarious MAD LIBS® game!

DREAM DATE

VERB ENDING IN "ING" _____

OCCUPATION _____

PLURAL NOUN _____

ADJECTIVE _____

ADJECTIVE _____

PART OF THE BODY _____

A PLACE _____

ADJECTIVE _____

A PLACE _____

ADJECTIVE _____

TYPE OF FOOD _____

TYPE OF LIQUID _____

ADJECTIVE _____

PART OF THE BODY _____

MAD LIBS

DREAM DATE

One day while he was _____ in the Riverdale High
                         VERB ENDING IN "ING"

library, Archie overheard Veronica tell Betty, "On my dream date with

Archie, he would pick me up in a/an _____-driven limousine
                                      OCCUPATION

with a bouquet of _____ and a box of _____
                     PLURAL NOUN   ADJECTIVE

chocolates on the passenger seat. Then we'd have dinner at the most

_____ restaurant in town and end the night walking hand in
   ADJECTIVE

_____ by (the) _____ in the moonlight." Betty
PART OF THE BODY   A PLACE

replied, "That sounds _____, but on my dream date, Archie
                          ADJECTIVE

would take me to an outdoor concert in (the) _____ for a/an
                                                A PLACE

_____ picnic with _____ and bottles of
   ADJECTIVE   TYPE OF FOOD

_____ and it would end with a ride in a/an _____-
TYPE OF LIQUID   ADJECTIVE

air balloon." Archie stuck his _____ around the corner and
                                  PART OF THE BODY

said, "You're both dreaming if you think I can afford to do either of

those dates!"

From ARCHIE® LOVES BETTY AND VERONICA® MAD LIBS® • TM and © 2014 Archie Comic Publications, Inc.
Published by Price Stern Sloan, an imprint of Penguin Group (USA) LLC, 345 Hudson Street, New York, NY 10014.

MAD LIBS® is fun to play with friends, but you can also play it by yourself! To begin with, DO NOT look at the story on the page below. Fill in the blanks on this page with the words called for. Then, using the words you have selected, fill in the blank spaces in the story.

Now you've created your own hilarious MAD LIBS® game!

HALF-BAKED

VERB _____

A PLACE _____

NOUN _____

TYPE OF LIQUID _____

ADJECTIVE _____

VERB _____

EXCLAMATION _____

PLURAL NOUN _____

NOUN _____

ADVERB _____

VERB ENDING IN "ING" _____

VERB (PAST TENSE) _____

ADJECTIVE _____

ADJECTIVE _____

NOUN _____

ADJECTIVE _____

A PLACE _____

VERB _____

Veronica decided to surprise Archie and _____ him a cake.
<small>VERB</small>

She found all the ingredients in (the) _____ and shooed away
<small>A PLACE</small>

Gaston the chef. While she melted chocolate in a pan on the

_____, she poured the flour, sugar, _____,
<small>NOUN</small>　　　　　　　　　　　　　　　　　　<small>TYPE OF LIQUID</small>

and eggs into a/an _____ bowl to _____ together.
<small>ADJECTIVE</small>　　　　　　　　<small>VERB</small>

"_____! I forgot to crack the _____ and now my
<small>EXCLAMATION</small>　　　　　　　　　　　<small>PLURAL NOUN</small>

batter is full of broken shells!" Just then, the _____ alarm
<small>NOUN</small>

started to beep _____. The chocolate was
<small>ADVERB</small>

_____! When Gaston _____ back
<small>VERB ENDING IN "ING"</small>　　　　　<small>VERB (PAST TENSE)</small>

into the kitchen, he found spilled batter and _____ smoke
<small>ADJECTIVE</small>

everywhere. Veronica cried, "Look at the _____ mess I've
<small>ADJECTIVE</small>

made . . . but I promised Archie a delicious homemade _____!"
<small>NOUN</small>

Gaston sighed and said, "It is better if you leave the baking to me, Miss

Veronica, otherwise I am _____ there might not be a/an
<small>ADJECTIVE</small>

_____ left in which to ever _____ anything ever
<small>A PLACE</small>　　　　　　　　　　　　　<small>VERB</small>

again!"

From ARCHIE® LOVES BETTY AND VERONICA® MAD LIBS® • TM and © 2014 Archie Comic Publications, Inc.
Published by Price Stern Sloan, an imprint of Penguin Group (USA) LLC, 345 Hudson Street, New York, NY 10014.

MAD LIBS® is fun to play with friends, but you can also play it by yourself! To begin with, DO NOT look at the story on the page below. Fill in the blanks on this page with the words called for. Then, using the words you have selected, fill in the blank spaces in the story.

Now you've created your own hilarious MAD LIBS® game!

THE BURGER TRAP

PART OF THE BODY (PLURAL) _____

ADJECTIVE _____

EXCLAMATION _____

ADJECTIVE _____

TYPE OF FOOD _____

PART OF THE BODY _____

NOUN _____

ADJECTIVE _____

PLURAL NOUN _____

VERB (PAST TENSE) _____

ADJECTIVE _____

NOUN _____

PART OF THE BODY (PLURAL) _____

TYPE OF FOOD _____

MAD LIBS®

THE BURGER TRAP

Jughead couldn't believe his _____! Waiting for
                                            PART OF THE BODY (PLURAL)

him outside his front door was a hot, _____ hamburger. And
                                               ADJECTIVE

at the end of the walkway was another one! And farther along down the

street, one more! "_____! This is the most _____ day
                     EXCLAMATION   ADJECTIVE

ever!" he said. The _____ trail stretched on ahead of him as far
                        TYPE OF FOOD

as his _____ could see. "Hmm, someone must have a hole in
        PART OF THE BODY

their lunch _____! I'll follow this burger trail and tell the
                  NOUN

_____ guy about it . . . but I better not let these _____
    ADJECTIVE   PLURAL NOUN

go to waste!" He _____ his way across town, gobbling
                      VERB (PAST TENSE)

down one burger after another, until the _____ trail ended . . .
                                     ADJECTIVE

at Ethel's _____! The door was decorated with pink
              NOUN

_____ for Valentine's Day, and it flew open to
PART OF THE BODY (PLURAL)

reveal Ethel waiting inside with more hamburgers. "Valentine's Day is

all about love . . . and there's nothing Jughead loves more than

_____!"
TYPE OF FOOD

MAD LIBS® is fun to play with friends, but you can also play it by yourself! To begin with, DO NOT look at the story on the page below. Fill in the blanks on this page with the words called for. Then, using the words you have selected, fill in the blank spaces in the story.

Now you've created your own hilarious MAD LIBS® game!

DON'T BE LATE!

ADJECTIVE _____

NOUN _____

VERB (PAST TENSE) _____

ADJECTIVE _____

NOUN _____

COLOR _____

NOUN _____

PART OF THE BODY (PLURAL) _____

NOUN _____

PART OF THE BODY _____

VERB (PAST TENSE) _____

ADJECTIVE _____

ARTICLE OF CLOTHING _____

ADJECTIVE _____

MAD LIBS
DON'T BE LATE!

Dear Diary,

Something very _____ happened tonight while I was
                    ADJECTIVE

dressing for my Valentine's Day _____ with Archie. Daddy
                                      NOUN

_____ in and said, "Hurry! You don't want to be
  VERB (PAST TENSE)

_____ and keep the young _____ waiting." I said,
   ADJECTIVE   NOUN

"Er . . . you know my date's with Archie, don't you?" "Yes, yes," he said.

He took a/an _____ dress from my _____. "This
                 COLOR   NOUN

matches your lovely blue _____. And make sure
                         PART OF THE BODY (PLURAL)

you wear your _____ the way Archie likes it!" I thought he
                  NOUN

had lost his _____! The last time Archie was here, he
               PART OF THE BODY

_____ a/an _____ vase and spilled paint on
   VERB (PAST TENSE)   ADJECTIVE

Daddy's brand-new _____. "But Daddy, you said
                    ARTICLE OF CLOTHING

you never wanted to see him again." Daddy said, "I don't . . . but I've

planned a/an _____ dinner with your mother and I'll even
                 ADJECTIVE

put up with Archie if it gets you out of the house for the evening!"

From ARCHIE® LOVES BETTY AND VERONICA® MAD LIBS® • TM and © 2014 Archie Comic Publications, Inc.
Published by Price Stern Sloan, an imprint of Penguin Group (USA) LLC, 345 Hudson Street, New York, NY 10014.

MAD LIBS® is fun to play with friends, but you can also play it by yourself! To begin with, DO NOT look at the story on the page below. Fill in the blanks on this page with the words called for. Then, using the words you have selected, fill in the blank spaces in the story.

Now you've created your own hilarious MAD LIBS® game!

MAD MOOSE

NOUN _____

A PLACE _____

VERB ENDING IN "ING" _____

ADJECTIVE _____

ANIMAL _____

PART OF THE BODY _____

ADJECTIVE _____

PLURAL NOUN _____

ADJECTIVE _____

NOUN _____

COLOR _____

ADVERB _____

VERB (PAST TENSE) _____

VERB _____

ADJECTIVE _____

ADJECTIVE _____

NUMBER _____

MAD☺LIBS®
MAD MOOSE

Moose was looking for a/an _____ on the shelves in
NOUN

the school _____ when he heard his girlfriend, Midge,
A PLACE

_____ in the next row. "Oh, that boy is just
VERB ENDING IN "ING"

_____ about me. He follows me everywhere I go like a
ADJECTIVE

lovesick _____ and wants to hold my _____ and give
ANIMAL   PART OF THE BODY

me _____ hugs. Last night, he gave me _____ from
ADJECTIVE   PLURAL NOUN

the garden and a/an _____ card that he made himself.
ADJECTIVE

And tonight, he's promised me a big box of _____ candy!"
NOUN

Moose's face turned _____ and he growled _____
COLOR   ADVERB

as he _____ over to Midge. "*Grr!* Tell me the name of
VERB (PAST TENSE)

the guy trying to _____ a move on you, Midge . . . I'm gonna
VERB

make him sorry he was ever _____!" "Oh, you don't have to
ADJECTIVE

be _____ about this boy," she said. "I was talking about the
ADJECTIVE

_____-year-old I babysit!"
NUMBER

From ARCHIE® LOVES BETTY AND VERONICA® MAD LIBS® • TM and © 2014 Archie Comic Publications, Inc.
Published by Price Stern Sloan, an imprint of Penguin Group (USA) LLC, 345 Hudson Street, New York, NY 10014.

MAD LIBS® is fun to play with friends, but you can also play it by yourself! To begin with, DO NOT look at the story on the page below. Fill in the blanks on this page with the words called for. Then, using the words you have selected, fill in the blank spaces in the story.

Now you've created your own hilarious MAD LIBS® game!

THE REGGIE RAFFLE

NOUN _____

NOUN _____

ADJECTIVE _____

ADJECTIVE _____

ADJECTIVE _____

NOUN _____

ADJECTIVE _____

PART OF THE BODY (PLURAL) _____

PLURAL NOUN _____

A PLACE _____

VERB _____

PART OF THE BODY _____

NOUN _____

EXCLAMATION _____

ADVERB _____

COLOR _____

PART OF THE BODY _____

NOUN _____

MAD LIBS®
THE REGGIE RAFFLE

Archie met up with Reggie, who was carrying a large _____
                                                        NOUN

bowl filled with folded pieces of _____. "It's for a/an
                                          NOUN

_____ Valentine's Day Dance raffle," Reggie explained.
   ADJECTIVE

"What's the _____ prize?" Archie asked. "Me!" Reggie said.
              ADJECTIVE

"It's the only _____ way I can think of to give all the girls an
                 ADJECTIVE

opportunity for a/an _____ with the _____ Reggie
                            NOUN   ADJECTIVE

Mantle!" Archie rolled his _____ and said, "You
                             PART OF THE BODY (PLURAL)

mean the girls are putting their _____ in the bowl? I'll
                                     PLURAL NOUN

believe it when I see it!" Later, at lunch in (the) _____,
                                                      A PLACE

Reggie announced that it was time to _____ the winner. He
                                          VERB

reached his _____ into the bowl and selected a/an
              PART OF THE BODY

_____. "_____?! Miss Beazley?" As all the girls
     NOUN   EXCLAMATION

started to laugh _____, Reggie read the rest of the slips. One
                    ADVERB

girl had written in the name of the _____-haired,
                                          COLOR

snaggle-_____ lunchroom lady instead of her own! "I guess
          PART OF THE BODY

you're not the _____ you thought you were, after all!" Archie
                  NOUN

laughed.

MAD LIBS® is fun to play with friends, but you can also play it by yourself! To begin with, DO NOT look at the story on the page below. Fill in the blanks on this page with the words called for. Then, using the words you have selected, fill in the blank spaces in the story.

Now you've created your own hilarious MAD LIBS® game!

BURGER LOVE

NOUN _____

PART OF THE BODY _____

NOUN _____

ADJECTIVE _____

TYPE OF FOOD _____

VERB (PAST TENSE) _____

VERB ENDING IN "ING" _____

PLURAL NOUN _____

VERB (PAST TENSE) _____

NOUN _____

NOUN _____

ADJECTIVE _____

ADJECTIVE _____

NOUN _____

TYPE OF FOOD _____

MAD LIBS

BURGER LOVE

According to a/an _____ in the *Riverdale Gazette*, Pop Tate
NOUN

was planning on making a special _____-shaped hamburger
PART OF THE BODY

for Valentine's Day. But Pop reported that one customer used every

_____ in the book to get more than his share of the
NOUN

_____-edition _____. "Jughead was waiting outside
ADJECTIVE   TYPE OF FOOD

when I opened the Chocklit Shoppe in the morning and

_____ two burgers. He came back a little later
VERB (PAST TENSE)

_____ one of his mother's hats and _____
VERB ENDING IN "ING"   PLURAL NOUN

and had two more. Then he _____ several more times,
VERB (PAST TENSE)

disguised as a/an _____ officer, a circus _____, a/an
NOUN   NOUN

_____-sea diver, a caped _____ hero, and a/an
ADJECTIVE   ADJECTIVE

_____ in a surgical mask. Why did I keep letting him have all
NOUN

those burgers? Well, Valentine's Day is about love, and Jughead sure

does love my _____!"
TYPE OF FOOD

From ARCHIE® LOVES BETTY AND VERONICA® MAD LIBS® • TM and © 2014 Archie Comic Publications, Inc.
Published by Price Stern Sloan, an imprint of Penguin Group (USA) LLC, 345 Hudson Street, New York, NY 10014.

MAD LIBS® is fun to play with friends, but you can also play it by yourself! To begin with, DO NOT look at the story on the page below. Fill in the blanks on this page with the words called for. Then, using the words you have selected, fill in the blank spaces in the story.

Now you've created your own hilarious MAD LIBS® game!

WHAT TO WEAR

ADJECTIVE _____

VERB ENDING IN "ING" _____

COLOR _____

PLURAL NOUN _____

ADJECTIVE _____

PLURAL NOUN _____

PLURAL NOUN _____

TYPE OF FOOD _____

TYPE OF LIQUID _____

ADJECTIVE _____

PERSON IN ROOM (MALE) _____

NUMBER _____

MAD LIBS®
WHAT TO WEAR

It was time for Veronica to get ready for her _____ date with
                                              ADJECTIVE

Archie. "Hmm, I wish I knew where we were going so I could decide

what to wear!" If they were going _____, she could
                                   VERB ENDING IN "ING"

wear her new _____ dancing _____. But Archie
             COLOR   PLURAL NOUN

had mentioned bowling, which would give her a chance to wear those

_____ new stretch _____ and matching bowling
   ADJECTIVE   PLURAL NOUN

_____! Of course, they could just be headed over to Pop's
  PLURAL NOUN

for a/an _____ and two glasses of _____, so she
         TYPE OF FOOD   TYPE OF LIQUID

could go _____ in a pair of comfy jeans and one of Daddy's
         ADJECTIVE

_____ Brothers shirts! When she finally went downstairs,
PERSON IN ROOM (MALE)

she asked Smithers if Archie had arrived. "Yes, Miss Veronica, but after

waiting for _____ hours while you dressed, he called Miss Betty
            NUMBER

and left with her."

From ARCHIE® LOVES BETTY AND VERONICA® MAD LIBS® • TM and © 2014 Archie Comic Publications, Inc.
Published by Price Stern Sloan, an imprint of Penguin Group (USA) LLC, 345 Hudson Street, New York, NY 10014.

MAD LIBS® is fun to play with friends, but you can also play it by yourself! To begin with, DO NOT look at the story on the page below. Fill in the blanks on this page with the words called for. Then, using the words you have selected, fill in the blank spaces in the story.

Now you've created your own hilarious MAD LIBS® game!

SURPRISE!

ADJECTIVE _____

ADJECTIVE _____

FIRST NAME (FEMALE) _____

FIRST NAME (MALE) _____

ADJECTIVE _____

NOUN _____

A PLACE _____

COLOR _____

PART OF THE BODY (PLURAL) _____

VERB _____

ADJECTIVE _____

ADJECTIVE _____

EXCLAMATION _____

VERB _____

"I've got the most _____ luck in the world!" Kevin said
                         ADJECTIVE

with a/an _____ sigh. "My cousin _____ is
          ADJECTIVE   FIRST NAME (FEMALE)

getting married the same night as the Valentine's Day Dance." "Oh no,

that means you and _____ won't be together on your
                    FIRST NAME (MALE)

first Valentine's!" Veronica said. But then she had a/an _____
                                                          ADJECTIVE

idea. The day before Valentine's Day, Veronica invited Kevin to her

_____. When he arrived, Kevin saw that (the) _____
    NOUN   A PLACE

was decorated with _____ streamers. _____
                      COLOR   PART OF THE BODY (PLURAL)

and the Archies, the gang's rock-and-_____ band, was set
                                      VERB

up to perform. "We felt so _____ that you were missing
                           ADJECTIVE

Valentine's Day with Devon, we arranged a/an _____ party
                                             ADJECTIVE

just for you guys!" Veronica said. "_____! You guys are great!
                                    EXCLAMATION

And, Devon, may I have the first _____?" Kevin asked.
                                 VERB

From ARCHIE® LOVES BETTY AND VERONICA® MAD LIBS® • TM and © 2014 Archie Comic Publications, Inc.
Published by Price Stern Sloan, an imprint of Penguin Group (USA) LLC, 345 Hudson Street, New York, NY 10014.

MAD LIBS® is fun to play with friends, but you can also play it by yourself! To begin with, DO NOT look at the story on the page below. Fill in the blanks on this page with the words called for. Then, using the words you have selected, fill in the blank spaces in the story.

Now you've created your own hilarious MAD LIBS® game!

LOVE AT FIRST BITE

VERB _____

NOUN _____

ADJECTIVE _____

NOUN _____

PART OF THE BODY _____

PART OF THE BODY _____

ADVERB _____

ADJECTIVE _____

VERB ENDING IN "ING" _____

NOUN _____

NOUN _____

ADJECTIVE _____

VERB _____

ADJECTIVE _____

NOUN _____

VERB _____

ADJECTIVE _____

ANIMAL _____

LOVE AT FIRST BITE

While out for a/an _____, Hot Dog and his owner, Jughead,
                     VERB

passed   by   Veronica's   _____.   Hot   Dog   heard   a/an
                            NOUN

_____ bark coming from the other side of the _____.
ADJECTIVE   NOUN

When he stuck his _____ through to see who was making the
                  PART OF THE BODY

noise, his _____ started to thump _____. It was
           PART OF THE BODY   ADVERB

FruFru, Veronica's prize pet French poodle . . . and she was the most

_____ dog he had ever seen! FruFru was _____
ADJECTIVE   VERB ENDING IN "ING"

at Smithers the _____, who was serving her dinner in a silver
                NOUN

_____. When Smithers noticed Hot Dog, he smiled and
NOUN

added a dish of _____ dog food so that the two dogs could
                ADJECTIVE

_____ together. Hot Dog couldn't believe his _____
VERB   ADJECTIVE

luck! But as he went to take his first _____, FruFru started to
                                       NOUN

_____ and snap at him. Hot Dog jumped back and hurried
VERB

away. She wasn't so _____ after all, especially when she acted
                    ADJECTIVE

like such a/an _____!
               ANIMAL

From ARCHIE® LOVES BETTY AND VERONICA® MAD LIBS® • TM and © 2014 Archie Comic Publications, Inc.
Published by Price Stern Sloan, an imprint of Penguin Group (USA) LLC, 345 Hudson Street, New York, NY 10014.

MAD LIBS® is fun to play with friends, but you can also play it by yourself! To begin with, DO NOT look at the story on the page below. Fill in the blanks on this page with the words called for. Then, using the words you have selected, fill in the blank spaces in the story.

Now you've created your own hilarious MAD LIBS® game!

BOWLED OVER

VERB ENDING IN "ING" _____

NOUN _____

ADJECTIVE _____

PLURAL NOUN _____

NOUN _____

ADJECTIVE _____

VERB (PAST TENSE) _____

NOUN _____

ADJECTIVE _____

PART OF THE BODY _____

ADVERB _____

NOUN _____

VERB _____

VERB ENDING IN "ING" _____

ADJECTIVE _____

MAD LIBS®
BOWLED OVER

One night at the Riverdale Lanes _____ alley, Archie
                                          VERB ENDING IN "ING"

was flirting with the two girls in the next _____. "Come on,
                                       NOUN

help me out, Jughead," Archie begged his _____ friend. "If I
                                    ADJECTIVE

wanted to hang out with _____, I would've stayed home
                              PLURAL NOUN

with my _____ and sister," Jughead replied. Archie picked up
                NOUN

his bowling ball and with a/an _____ smile and wink at the
                                ADJECTIVE

girls, _____ up to the line to throw his _____.
        VERB (PAST TENSE)   NOUN

He took a/an _____ step forward, then another, and then he
                ADJECTIVE

felt his _____ slip on the slick floor. He swung the ball
            PART OF THE BODY

_____, and both he and it went flying through the air. Archie
    ADVERB

fell to the _____. The ball began to _____, and the
            NOUN   VERB

girls ran away, _____ in fear. Jughead said, "Well, you
            VERB ENDING IN "ING"

were trying to make them notice you and they did . . . just not in a/an

_____ way."
  ADJECTIVE

From ARCHIE® LOVES BETTY AND VERONICA® MAD LIBS® • TM and © 2014 Archie Comic Publications, Inc.
Published by Price Stern Sloan, an imprint of Penguin Group (USA) LLC, 345 Hudson Street, New York, NY 10014.

MAD LIBS® is fun to play with friends, but you can also play it by yourself! To begin with, DO NOT look at the story on the page below. Fill in the blanks on this page with the words called for. Then, using the words you have selected, fill in the blank spaces in the story.

Now you've created your own hilarious MAD LIBS® game!

WHAT A CARD!

VERB (PAST TENSE) _____

NOUN _____

ADVERB _____

PART OF THE BODY _____

PERSON IN ROOM (MALE) _____

COLOR _____

PART OF THE BODY (PLURAL) _____

ADJECTIVE _____

PART OF THE BODY _____

NOUN _____

ADJECTIVE _____

VERB _____

ADVERB _____

NOUN _____

FIRST NAME (FEMALE) _____

MAD LIBS
WHAT A CARD!

After the Valentine's Day Dance, Betty _____ in her
                                            VERB (PAST TENSE)

diary, "I love Veronica, but sometimes that best _____ of mine
                                                             NOUN

thinks she can get away with anything just because she's _____
                                                                        ADVERB

rich! The whole gang had decided that this year we would only give

_____-made cards for the holiday. I made the best card for
PART OF THE BODY

_____, with lots of _____ and red
      PERSON IN ROOM (MALE)   COLOR

_____, and a/an _____ poem I wrote just
PART OF THE BODY (PLURAL)   ADJECTIVE

for him. My card from Archie was _____-painted on the
                                           PART OF THE BODY

wings of a glider shaped like a/an _____. But Veronica's cards
                                           NOUN

were _____! "You made these?" I said with a/an _____.
        ADJECTIVE   VERB

"Well, not _____," she admitted. "But they were supposed to
            ADVERB

be homemade, Veronica!" "They are! Made at the _____ of
                                           NOUN

my designer, Madame _____."
                      FIRST NAME (FEMALE)

MAD LIBS® is fun to play with friends, but you can also play it by yourself! To begin with, DO NOT look at the story on the page below. Fill in the blanks on this page with the words called for. Then, using the words you have selected, fill in the blank spaces in the story.

Now you've created your own hilarious MAD LIBS® game!

E-LOVE

ADJECTIVE _____

ADJECTIVE _____

PERSON IN ROOM (MALE) _____

NOUN _____

ADJECTIVE _____

NOUN _____

VERB _____

A PLACE _____

NOUN _____

ADJECTIVE _____

ADJECTIVE _____

ADVERB _____

NOUN _____

NOUN _____

FIRST NAME (FEMALE) _____

MAD LIBS®
E-LOVE

"You joined a/an _____ dating service?" Reggie asked. "That's
 ADJECTIVE

right. I got sick and _____ of waiting for _____
 ADJECTIVE PERSON IN ROOM (MALE)

to ask me out!" Ethel replied. The following week, Reggie asked her if

she had been on an Internet _____ yet. "No, but I did find a
 NOUN

boy who sounds _____! He's very shy about posting his
 ADJECTIVE

_____ online, but we've been e-mailing and agreed to
 NOUN

_____ tomorrow at (the) _____." The next day at
 VERB A PLACE

Pop's, the only _____ there was Jughead. "Excuse me, but did
 NOUN

you see my date?" she asked him. "No," Jughead said as he took a bite

out of a/an _____ burger, "but if he's your date, he's probably
 ADJECTIVE

_____!" Just then Reggie came in, laughing _____.
 ADJECTIVE ADVERB

"The _____ is on you, Jug! I signed you up for that dating
 NOUN

service . . . and it made you a/an _____ with
 NOUN

_____!" "Me? It sounds like you're the one who
 FIRST NAME (FEMALE)

made the date, Reggie!" Jughead said.

From ARCHIE® LOVES BETTY AND VERONICA® MAD LIBS® • TM and © 2014 Archie Comic Publications, Inc.
Published by Price Stern Sloan, an imprint of Penguin Group (USA) LLC, 345 Hudson Street, New York, NY 10014.

MAD LIBS® is fun to play with friends, but you can also play it by yourself! To begin with, DO NOT look at the story on the page below. Fill in the blanks on this page with the words called for. Then, using the words you have selected, fill in the blank spaces in the story.

Now you've created your own hilarious MAD LIBS® game!

HIDE-AND-SEEK

FIRST NAME (MALE) _____

VERB _____

NOUN _____

ADJECTIVE _____

PERSON IN ROOM (FEMALE) _____

ADJECTIVE _____

NOUN _____

VERB _____

ANIMAL _____

VERB _____

NOUN _____

NOUN _____

SAME NOUN _____

VERB _____

VERB (PAST TENSE) _____

ANIMAL (PLURAL) _____

NOUN _____

ADJECTIVE _____

MAD LIBS®
HIDE-AND-SEEK

Jughead sent _____ a text message: "You better
_{FIRST NAME (MALE)}

_____! Betty and Veronica found out you asked them both to
_{VERB}

be your _____ on Valentine's Day!" Archie's message back
_{NOUN}

read, "How could I make such a/an _____ mistake? How mad
_{ADJECTIVE}

are they?" But the next text was from _____ and it
_{PERSON IN ROOM (FEMALE)}

was _____: "How dare you, you rotten _____!" The
_{ADJECTIVE}   _{NOUN}

one after that was from Betty: "There's nowhere you can _____,
_{VERB}

you _____!" Jughead texted, "Better _____, pal!
_{ANIMAL}   _{VERB}

Moose just reported the girls are headed to your _____!"
_{NOUN}

Archie replied, "Betty's coming to the front _____! Veronica's
_{NOUN}

at the back _____! I'm trapped!" After a long silence, Jughead
_{SAME NOUN}

wrote, "Did you _____?" Archie replied, "No, I
_{VERB}

_____ through the skylight to the roof!" Jughead
_{VERB (PAST TENSE)}

wrote back: "But it's raining cats and _____!" "I'd rather
_{ANIMAL (PLURAL)}

risk being out here and catching a/an _____ than being caught
_{NOUN}

by two _____ girls!" Archie replied.
_{ADJECTIVE}

From ARCHIE® LOVES BETTY AND VERONICA® MAD LIBS® • TM and © 2014 Archie Comic Publications, Inc.
Published by Price Stern Sloan, an imprint of Penguin Group (USA) LLC, 345 Hudson Street, New York, NY 10014.

MAD LIBS® is fun to play with friends, but you can also play it by yourself! To begin with, DO NOT look at the story on the page below. Fill in the blanks on this page with the words called for. Then, using the words you have selected, fill in the blank spaces in the story.

Now you've created your own hilarious MAD LIBS® game!

DRESS FOR SUCCESS

ADJECTIVE _____

OCCUPATION _____

CELEBRITY (LAST NAME) _____

EXCLAMATION _____

COLOR _____

ADJECTIVE _____

PERSON IN ROOM (MALE) _____

ADJECTIVE _____

A PLACE _____

PART OF THE BODY (PLURAL) _____

ADVERB _____

COLOR _____

ADJECTIVE _____

FIRST NAME (FEMALE) _____

NUMBER _____

VERB _____

PERSON IN ROOM _____

MAD LIBS

DRESS FOR SUCCESS

Veronica came home from the dress shop with a/an _____
ADJECTIVE

new dress by _____ Claude St. _____.
OCCUPATION   CELEBRITY (LAST NAME)

"_____! Every girl at the party will be _____ with
EXCLAMATION   COLOR

envy when they see me in this!" On the night of the _____
ADJECTIVE

party, Veronica and her date, _____, were the last to
PERSON IN ROOM (MALE)

arrive so she could make a/an _____ entrance! As she
ADJECTIVE

walked into (the) _____, she felt all _____
A PLACE   PART OF THE BODY (PLURAL)

turn her way. But then someone started to laugh _____
ADVERB

and soon enough, everyone else joined in. Veronica turned

_____ from embarrassment. What was so _____?
COLOR   ADJECTIVE

Then she saw _____ and two other girls . . . and they
FIRST NAME (FEMALE)

were all wearing her dress! "But it's supposed to be _____ of a
NUMBER

kind!" Veronica said with a/an _____. "Maybe it's one of a
VERB

kind where you shop, but at _____'s Department Store,
PERSON IN ROOM

they've got dozens of them," Betty said.

MAD LIBS® is fun to play with friends, but you can also play it by yourself! To begin with, DO NOT look at the story on the page below. Fill in the blanks on this page with the words called for. Then, using the words you have selected, fill in the blank spaces in the story.

Now you've created your own hilarious MAD LIBS® game!

LOVE TRIANGLE PLUS ONE

NOUN _____

VERB _____

NOUN _____

ADJECTIVE _____

PART OF THE BODY _____

ADVERB _____

ADJECTIVE _____

ADJECTIVE _____

VERB _____

NOUN _____

The *Riverdale High Weekly News* _____ column reports that
                                        NOUN

Betty and Veronica have made a schedule to date Archie. "The only

thing Betty and I ever _____ about is Archie, and now we
                              VERB

don't ever have to have another _____," Veronica said. "Now
                                       NOUN

we don't have to waste time playing _____ tricks on each
                                           ADJECTIVE

other to see who gets Archie's _____. Now it's share and share
                                   PART OF THE BODY

_____," Betty said. Veronica added that she and Betty had
   ADVERB

been _____ friends forever, saying, "We agree on everything
       ADJECTIVE

except Archie." "Besides, last night, he told me he was _____
                                                            ADJECTIVE

and couldn't make our date, but Midge said she saw him later at a /an

_____-in movie with Cheryl Blossom! So Veronica and I have
   VERB

to work together as a/an _____ . . . because neither of us will
                              NOUN

ever date him if she moves in on him first!"

MAD LIBS® is fun to play with friends, but you can also play it by yourself! To begin with, DO NOT look at the story on the page below. Fill in the blanks on this page with the words called for. Then, using the words you have selected, fill in the blank spaces in the story.

Now you've created your own hilarious MAD LIBS® game!

DOUBLE DATE

NUMBER _____

NOUN _____

TYPE OF FOOD _____

VERB _____

CELEBRITY (FEMALE) _____

NOUN _____

ANIMAL _____

NOUN _____

VERB ENDING IN "ING" _____

PLURAL NOUN _____

VERB (PAST TENSE) _____

ADJECTIVE _____

PLURAL NOUN _____

ADVERB _____

PERSON IN ROOM (FEMALE) _____

EXCLAMATION _____

ADJECTIVE _____

MAD LIBS
DOUBLE DATE

Moose and Jughead were at the multiplex to see *Return of the*

_____-*Armed* _____-*Man*. As they waited in line for
　　　NUMBER　　　　　　　　　NOUN

_____, they were surprised to see Archie _____ out
　TYPE OF FOOD　　　　　　　　　　　　　　　　　　　VERB

of one of the theaters showing the new _____ movie
　　　　　　　　　　　　　　　　　CELEBRITY (FEMALE)

and into the one right beside it showing the new _____ about
　　　　　　　　　　　　　　　　　　　　　　NOUN

the boy and the _____ trapped together on a/an
　　　　　　　　ANIMAL

_____. A few moments later, he came _____
　　NOUN　　　　　　　　　　　　　　　VERB ENDING IN "ING"

out of the second theater and back into the first. Then, as Jughead was

asking for _____ and butter on his popcorn, Archie
　　　　PLURAL NOUN

_____ back out and over to the candy counter. He was
VERB (PAST TENSE)

totally _____ and out of breath. "Seeing two movies at once?"
　　　ADJECTIVE

Jughead asked. "No, I'm out on two _____ at
　　　　　　　　　　　　　　　　PLURAL NOUN

once . . . I _____ asked out both _____ and
　　　　ADVERB　　　　　　　　　PERSON IN ROOM (FEMALE)

Veronica for tonight. _____, I never knew double dating was
　　　　　　　　　EXCLAMATION

so _____!"
　　ADJECTIVE

MAD LIBS® is fun to play with friends, but you can also play it by yourself! To begin with, DO NOT look at the story on the page below. Fill in the blanks on this page with the words called for. Then, using the words you have selected, fill in the blank spaces in the story.

Now you've created your own hilarious MAD LIBS® game!

A BRIEF HISTORY OF LOVE

ADJECTIVE _____

NOUN _____

ADJECTIVE _____

ADJECTIVE _____

PART OF THE BODY _____

ADVERB _____

PLURAL NOUN _____

NOUN _____

ADJECTIVE _____

TYPE OF FOOD _____

ADJECTIVE _____

ADJECTIVE _____

ADJECTIVE _____

VERB ENDING IN "ING" _____

MAD LIBS

A BRIEF HISTORY OF LOVE

Hello, Dilton Doily here with a/an _____ history of

ADJECTIVE

love and Valentine's Day. Many believe it is a/an _____

NOUN

invented by the greeting-card industry, but it actually dates back to

_____-times and is in honor of Saint Valentine. He was

ADJECTIVE

known for helping couples get _____. Even though many

ADJECTIVE

people believe that he invented the chocolate _____, that

PART OF THE BODY

is _____ untrue. The British started the tradition of giving

ADVERB

bouquets of _____, gifts, and sweets to your special

PLURAL NOUN

_____. It has become the most _____ day of the year

NOUN   ADJECTIVE

for chocolates. It is the one day guys better have _____ and

TYPE OF FOOD

flowers for their _____ girl. Because if history teaches us just

ADJECTIVE

one _____ lesson, it's that nothing will turn a day of love and

ADJECTIVE

peace into a/an _____ war faster than _____!

ADJECTIVE   VERB ENDING IN "ING"

MAD LIBS® is fun to play with friends, but you can also play it by yourself! To begin with, DO NOT look at the story on the page below. Fill in the blanks on this page with the words called for. Then, using the words you have selected, fill in the blank spaces in the story.

Now you've created your own hilarious MAD LIBS® game!

FLOWER POWER

EXCLAMATION _____

ADVERB _____

ADJECTIVE _____

PART OF THE BODY _____

A PLACE _____

ADJECTIVE _____

NOUN _____

PERSON IN ROOM (FEMALE) _____

NOUN _____

VEHICLE (PLURAL) _____

PLURAL NOUN _____

PLURAL NOUN _____

ADJECTIVE _____

PART OF THE BODY _____

VERB _____

PART OF THE BODY (PLURAL) _____

ADJECTIVE _____

MAD LIBS
FLOWER POWER

"_____, that's some bundle of buds, bud," Jughead said.

EXCLAMATION

Archie looked _____ at the bouquet of _____

ADVERB ADJECTIVE

flowers in his _____ and said, "I picked every single one

PART OF THE BODY

myself from my mother's _____. Then I trimmed them to

A PLACE

a/an _____ length and tied them together with a silk

ADJECTIVE

_____ . . . all for beautiful _____!" But

NOUN PERSON IN ROOM (FEMALE)

when Archie got to Veronica's _____ to give her the flowers,

NOUN

he spotted delivery _____ from all the local florist shops

VEHICLE (PLURAL)

already there. "So many gifts from my _____," Veronica

PLURAL NOUN

exclaimed. Archie could tell that all these expensive _____

PLURAL NOUN

would put his _____ batch of flowers to shame. He tried to

ADJECTIVE

hide them behind his _____, but Veronica saw them and

PART OF THE BODY

said, "Did you _____ these yourself?" Archie began to

VERB

apologize, but Veronica grabbed them out of his _____

PART OF THE BODY (PLURAL)

and said, "Oh, Archiekins, these are the most _____ flowers

ADJECTIVE

of all!"

From ARCHIE® LOVES BETTY AND VERONICA® MAD LIBS® • TM and © 2014 Archie Comic Publications, Inc.
Published by Price Stern Sloan, an imprint of Penguin Group (USA) LLC, 345 Hudson Street, New York, NY 10014.

MAD LIBS® is fun to play with friends, but you can also play it by yourself! To begin with, DO NOT look at the story on the page below. Fill in the blanks on this page with the words called for. Then, using the words you have selected, fill in the blank spaces in the story.

Now you've created your own hilarious MAD LIBS® game!

HYPNOTIC LOVE

PLURAL NOUN _____

PART OF THE BODY _____

ADJECTIVE _____

EXCLAMATION _____

ADVERB _____

PART OF THE BODY (PLURAL) _____

ADJECTIVE _____

VERB _____

SAME VERB _____

ADJECTIVE _____

PART OF THE BODY (PLURAL) _____

ADVERB _____

SILLY WORD _____

PART OF THE BODY (PLURAL) _____

NOUN _____

PART OF THE BODY _____

NOUN _____

ADJECTIVE _____

MAD LIBS
HYPNOTIC LOVE

"I've been practicing hypnotism. Do any of you _____

PLURAL NOUN

want to let me _____-wash you?" Archie asked. "Not me! I

PART OF THE BODY

don't want you to see what's inside my _____ brain," Jughead

ADJECTIVE

said. "_____! He'd have to find it first," Reggie said

EXCLAMATION

_____. "I'll volunteer, Archie," Betty said. "Okay, Betty, look

ADVERB

deep into my _____! You can hear only my

PART OF THE BODY (PLURAL)

_____ voice! You will do only as I _____!" "Yes,

ADJECTIVE   _VERB_

Archie, only as you _____!" Betty repeated. "When I say the

SAME VERB

_____ word and snap my _____, you

ADJECTIVE   _PART OF THE BODY (PLURAL)_

will fall _____ in love with me! _____!" With that,

ADVERB   _SILLY WORD_

Betty fell into Archie's _____ and started to kiss his

PART OF THE BODY (PLURAL)

_____. "Wow, Archie really did _____-wash Betty!"

NOUN   _PART OF THE BODY_

Jughead said. But Betty winked and whispered, "Not really, but I don't

have to be under a/an _____ to act like I'm _____

NOUN   _ADJECTIVE_

about Archie!"

This book is published by

PSS!

PRICE STERN SLOAN

whose other splendid titles include
such literary classics as